Published by Concordia Publishing House
3558 S. Jefferson Avenue, St. Louis, MO 63118-3968
Illustrations copyright © 2006 Guy Porfirio

Manufactured in China

1 2 3 4 5 6 7 8 9 10   15 14 13 12 11 10 09 08 07 06

A Christmas Carol
by Martin Luther

From Heaven Above

Illustrated by Guy Porfirio

CONCORDIA PUBLISHING HOUSE • SAINT LOUIS

And, lo, the angel of the Lord came upon them, and the
glory of the Lord shone round about them: and they were sore
afraid. And the angel said unto them, Fear not: for, behold, I bring
you good tidings of great joy, which shall be to all people. For unto
you is born this day in the city of David a Saviour, which is
Christ the Lord. And this shall be a sign unto you; Ye shall find the
babe wrapped in swaddling clothes, lying in a manger.

And suddenly there was with the angel a multitude of the
heavenly host praising God, and saying, Glory to God in the
highest, and on earth peace, good will toward men.

Luke 2:9–14 (KJV)

"From heav'n above to earth I come
To bear good news to ev'ry home;
Glad tidings of great joy I bring
Whereof I now will say and sing:

"To you this night is born a child
Of Mary, chosen virgin mild;
This little child of lowly birth
Shall be the joy of all the earth.

"This is the Christ, our God Most High,
Who hears your sad and bitter cry;
He will Himself your Savior be
From all your sins to set you free.

"He will on you the gifts bestow
Prepared by God for all below,
That in His kingdom, bright and fair,
You may with us His glory share.

"These are the signs that you shall mark:
The swaddling clothes and manger dark.
There you will find the infant laid
By whom the heav'ns and earth were made."

How glad we'll be to find it so!
Then with the shepherds let us go
To see what God for us has done
In sending us His own dear Son.

Come here, my friends, lift up your eyes,
And see what in the manger lies.
Who is this child, so young and fair?
It is the Christ Child lying there.

Welcome to earth, O noble Guest,
Through whom the sinful world is blest!
You came to share my misery
That You might share Your joy with me.

Ah, Lord, though You created all,
How weak You are, so poor and small,
That You should choose to lay Your head
Where lowly cattle lately fed!

Were earth a thousand times as fair
And set with gold and jewels rare,
It would be far too poor and small
A cradle for the Lord of all.

Instead of soft and silken stuff
You have but hay and straw so rough
On which as King, so rich and great,
To be enthroned in royal state.

Ah, dearest Jesus, holy Child,
Prepare a bed, soft, undefiled,
A quiet chamber set apart
For You to dwell within my heart.

My heart for very joy must leap;
My lips no more can silence keep.
I, too, must sing with joyful tongue
The sweetest ancient cradlesong:

Glory to God in highest heav'n,
Who unto us His Son has giv'n!
While angels sing with pious mirth
A glad new year to all the earth.

From Heaven Above

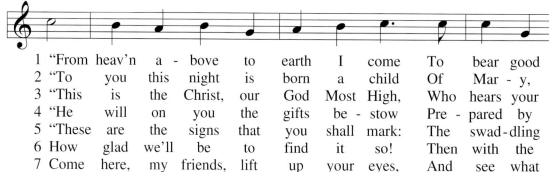

1 "From heav'n a- bove to earth I come To bear good
2 "To you this night is born a child Of Mar - y,
3 "This is the Christ, our God Most High, Who hears your
4 "He will on you the gifts be - stow Pre - pared by
5 "These are the signs that you shall mark: The swad - dling
6 How glad we'll be to find it so! Then with the
7 Come here, my friends, lift up your eyes, And see what

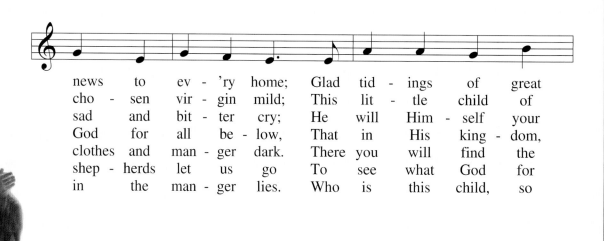

news to ev - 'ry home; Glad tid - ings of great
cho - sen vir - gin mild; This lit - tle child of
sad and bit - ter cry; He will Him - self your
God for all be - low, That in His king - dom,
clothes and man - ger dark. There you will find the
shep - herds let us go To see what God for
in the man - ger lies. Who is this child, so

joy I bring, Where - of I now will say and sing:
low - ly birth Shall be the joy of all the earth.
Sav - ior be From all your sins to set you free.
bright and fair, You may with us His glo - ry share.
in - fant laid By whom the heav'ns and earth were made."
us has done In send - ing us His own dear Son.
young and fair? It is the Christ Child ly - ing there.

Text: Martin Luther, 1483–1546; tr. Catherine Winkworth, 1827–78, alt.
Tune: VOM HIMMEL HOCH, *Geistliche Lieder*, Leipzig, 1539, ed. Valten Schumann

8 Wel - come to earth, O no - ble Guest, Through whom the
9 Ah, Lord, though You cre - at - ed all, How weak You
10 Were earth a thou - sand times as fair And set with
11 In - stead of soft and silk - en stuff You have but
12 Ah, dear - est Je - sus, ho - ly Child, Pre - pare a
13 My heart for ver - y joy must leap; My lips no
14 Glo - ry to God in high - est heav'n, Who un - to

sin - ful world is blest! You came to share my
are, so poor and small, That You should choose to
gold and jew - els rare, It would be far too
hay and straw so rough On which as King, so
bed, soft, un - de - filed, A qui - et cham - ber
more can si - lence keep. I, too, must sing with
us His Son has giv'n! While an - gels sing with

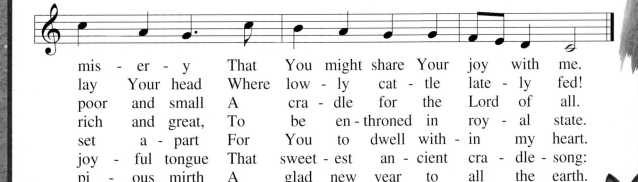

mis - er - y That You might share Your joy with me.
lay Your head Where low - ly cat - tle late - ly fed!
poor and small A cra - dle for the Lord of all.
rich and great, To be en - throned in roy - al state.
set a - part For You to dwell with - in my heart.
joy - ful tongue That sweet - est an - cient cra - dle - song:
pi - ous mirth A glad new year to all the earth.